LITERARY DEVICES
Reading Skills Series

• • • • • • • • • • • • • • • • •

Written by Brenda Vance Rollins, Ed. D.

GRADES 5 - 8
Reading Levels 3 - 4

Classroom Complete Press

P.O. Box 19729
San Diego, CA 92159
Tel: 1-800-663-3609 | Fax: 1-800-663-3608
Email: service@classroomcompletepress.com

www.classroomcompletepress.com

ISBN13: 978-155319-485-9

© 2010

Critical Thinking Skills

Literary Devices

Skills For Critical Thinking		1	2	3	4	5	6	7	8	9	10	11	12
LEVEL 1 Remembering	Define, Duplicate, List, Memorize, Recall, Repeat, Reproduce, State	✓	✓	✓	✓	✓	✓	✓	✓	✓	✓	✓	✓
LEVEL 2 Understanding	Classify, Describe, Discuss, Explain, Identify, Locate, Recognize	✓	✓	✓	✓	✓	✓	✓	✓	✓	✓	✓	✓
LEVEL 3 Applying	Choose, Demonstrate, Dramatize, Employ, Illustrate, Interpret, Operate, Write	✓	✓	✓	✓	✓	✓	✓	✓	✓	✓	✓	✓
LEVEL 4 Analysing	Appraise, Compare, Contrast, Criticize, Differentiate, Discriminate, Distinguish, Examine	✓	✓	✓	✓	✓	✓	✓	✓	✓	✓	✓	✓
LEVEL 5 Evaluating	Argue, Defend, Judge, Select, Support, Value, Decide, Evaluate	✓		✓	✓		✓			✓	✓		✓
LEVEL 6 Creating	Assemble, Construct, Create, Design, Develop, Formulate, Write.	✓	✓	✓	✓	✓	✓	✓	✓	✓	✓	✓	✓

Based on Bloom's Taxonomy

Contents

● ● ● ● ● ● ● ● ● ● ● ● ● ● ●

✔ **6 BONUS** Activity Pages! **Additional worksheets for your students**

FREE!

- Go to our website: **www.classroomcompletepress.com/bonus**
- Enter item CC1117
- Enter pass code CC1117D for Activity Pages.

Assessment Rubric

Literary Devices

Student's Name: _____   Assignment: _____   Level: _____

6 Exceptional Reader	An enthusiastic and reflective reader who enjoys pursuing own reading interests independently; is capable of reading in all content areas, can read a wide range and variety of materials including advanced materials, able to evaluate evidence drawn from a variety of sources. Is developing critical awareness as a reader. Has control of a variety of reading strategies (context clues, inferences, conclusions, main idea, fact & opinion, sequencing) to derive meaning.
5 Strong Reader	A self-motivated, confident reader who pursues own interests through reading. Capable of reading in all content areas and of locating and drawing on a variety of resources to research a topic independently. Uses multiple strategies (context clues, inferences, conclusions, main idea, fact & opinion, sequencing) to derive meaning. Begins to make predictions and draw inferences from books and stories read independently.
4 Competent Reader	A reader who feels comfortable with books. Is generally able to read silently and is developing confidence as a reader. Selects books independently, but still needs help with unfamiliar material. Uses some strategies to derive meaning.
3 Developing Reader	Is developing fluency as a reader and reads some books with confidence. Usually most comfortable with reading short books with simple narrative and/or with pictures. Relies on re-reading favorite or familiar books. Needs help with reading in the content areas, especially using reference and information books. Has growing ability to use a variety of strategies to derive meaning.
2 Emergent Reader	Chooses to read very easy and familiar material. Has difficulty with unfamiliar material, yet is usually able to read own writing. Gaining awareness of letters and their sounds. Needs a great deal of support with reading in all content areas. Beginning to use one or more strategies when reading. Enjoys being read to and participates in shared reading.
1 Pre-Reader	Enjoys being read to. Looks at pictures in books but does not yet make the connection to print. Watches and listens during shared reading rather than participates. Limited knowledge of letters and sounds. Has limited experience as a reader. Prior schooling may have been limited or interrupted.

STRENGTHS:

WEAKNESSES:

NEXT STEPS:

Literary Devices CC1117

Teacher Guide

Our resource has been created for ease of use by both TEACHERS and STUDENTS alike.

Introduction

This study of literary devices is designed to make the language of storytelling more useful to upper-elementary students. The goal of this workbook is to help learners know and use literary devices to examine the meaning and purpose of different types of literature. Through a mixture of narration and age appropriate learning activities, this book enables students to examine and understand the "building blocks" of all good stories. Also, with the study of literary devices comes the increased desire and ability to write well-balanced stories of their own.

Throughout *Literary Devices*, important concepts are emphasized and discussed. Definitions of important terms and many opportunities to practice the skills being taught, make this book user-friendly and easy to understand. In addition, the objectives used in this book are structured using Bloom's Taxonomy of Learning to ensure educational appropriateness.

How Is Our Resource Organized?

STUDENT HANDOUTS

Reading passages and **activities** (*in the form of reproducible worksheets*) make up the majority of our resource. The reading passages present important grade-appropriate information and concepts related to the topic. Embedded in each passage are one or more questions that ensure students understand what they have read.

For each reading passage there are **BEFORE YOU READ** activities and **AFTER YOU READ** activities.

- The BEFORE YOU READ activities prepare students for reading by setting a purpose for reading. They stimulate background knowledge and experience, and guide students to make connections between what they know and what they will learn. Important concepts and vocabulary from the chapters are also presented.
- The AFTER YOU READ activities check students' comprehension of the concepts presented in the reading

passage and extend their learning. Students are asked to give thoughtful consideration of the reading passage through creative and evaluative short-answer questions, research, and extension activities.

Writing Tasks are included to further develop students' thinking skills and understanding of the concepts. The **Assessment Rubric** (*page 4*) is a useful tool for evaluating students' responses to many of the activities in our resource. The **Comprehension Quiz** (*page 48*) can be used for either a follow-up review or assessment at the completion of the unit.

PICTURE CUES

This resource contains three main types of pages, each with a different purpose and use. A **Picture Cue** at the top of each page shows, at a glance, what the page is for.

 Teacher Guide
- Information and tools for the teacher

 Student Handout
- Reproducible worksheets and activities

 Easy Marking™ Answer Key
- Answers for student activities

EASY MARKING™ ANSWER KEY

Marking students' worksheets is fast and easy with this **Answer Key**. Answers are listed in columns – just line up the column with its corresponding worksheet, as shown, and see how every question matches up with its answer!

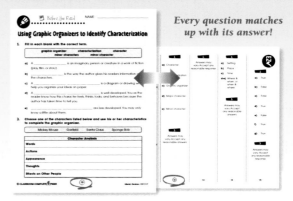

Every question matches up with its answer!

Bloom's Taxonomy* for Reading Comprehension

The activities in this resource engage and build the full range of thinking skills that are essential for students' reading comprehension. Based on the six levels of thinking in Bloom's Taxonomy, assignments are given that challenge students to not only recall what they have read, but move beyond this to understand the text through higher-order thinking. By using higher-order skills of applying, analysing, evaluating, and creating, students become active readers, drawing more meaning from the text, and applying and extending their learning in more sophisticated ways.

Our **Literary Devices Book** is an effective tool for any Language Arts program. Whether it is used in whole or in part, or adapted to meet individual student needs, this resource provides teachers with the important questions to ask, interesting content, which promote creative and meaningful learning.

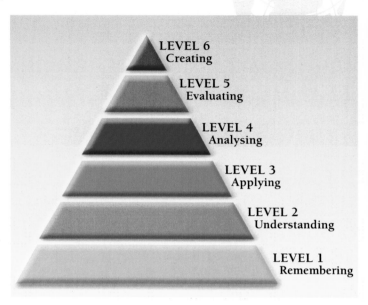

BLOOM'S TAXONOMY: 6 LEVELS OF THINKING

Bloom's Taxonomy is a widely used tool by educators for classifying learning objectives, and is based on the work of Benjamin Bloom.

Vocabulary

LITERARY DEVICES - the building blocks of storytelling.

CHARACTER - an imaginary person or creature in a work of fiction (play, film, or story).

CHARACTERIZATION - the way the author gives his readers information about the characters.

GRAPHIC ORGANIZER - a diagram or drawing which help you organize your ideas on paper.

SETTING - the time and location in which a story takes place.

NARRATIVE - any written work that tells a story, such as a short story, a novel, or a play.

PLOT - plan of action for a story, play, or movie.

INTRODUCTION OR OPENING OF A PLOT - describes the characters and the setting of the story.

RISING ACTION OF A PLOT - when readers find out more about the main characters and conflicts are introduced.

CLIMAX OF A PLOT - the "high point" of a story, when the major conflicts end up in some kind of final showdown (a fight, an argument, physical action, or a very tense emotional moment).

FALLING ACTION OF A PLOT - deals with the results of the climax.

RESOLUTION - a tying-up of all the loose ends left in the story.

FIVE STAGES OF PLOT DEVELOPMENT - introduction, rising action, climax, falling action, and resolution.

CONFLICT - the struggle between the opposing forces in a story.

THEME OF ANY STORY - the main idea or point that the author is trying to tell the audience. The theme refers to the entire message that the writer is trying to send through his story, through the use of characterization, action, and images.

AESOP'S FABLES - short tales that were written long ago for the purpose of teaching morals or lessons about life.

POINT OF VIEW - the way a story gets told and who tells it.

FIRST PERSON POINT OF VIEW - a character in the story is the narrator. This character is telling the story. The narrator uses the pronouns I, me, and we.

THIRD PERSON POINT OF VIEW - the story is being told by an outside observer (someone who is not in the story). The author uses the pronouns he, she, and they.

FORESHADOWING - when an author mentions or hints at something that will happen later in the story.

FLASHBACKS - when an author refers back to an event that has already taken place in the story.

IRONY - an expression in which the intended meaning of the words is the direct opposite of their usual sense.

VERBAL IRONY - using words to be ironic.

SITUATIONAL IRONY - when a set of circumstances or a result is the opposite of what might be expected.

LITERARY SYMBOLISM - when an object in a story, play, or movie stands for a feeling, idea, or concept.

Characterization

1. **Match the meaning on the right with its term on the left.**

A literary devices

B character

C characterization

D 5 methods of characterization

E major character

F minor character

1 1. the character's physical appearance (how the character looks); 2. the character's thoughts (what the character thinks); 3. the character's actions (what the character does); 4. the character's speech (what the character says); and 5. the character's interactions with other characters in the story (how the other characters react to him or her).

2 undeveloped characters

3 well-developed characters

4 an imaginary person or creature in a work of fiction (play, film, or story)

5 the building blocks of storytelling

6 the way the author gives his readers information about the characters

2. **Choose a well-developed character in a book you have read and answer the following questions about him or her.**

a) What is the character's name?_____

b) What is the character's physical appearance? (how he or she looks)

_____

c) What are some things the character does?

_____

d) What are some things the character says?

_____

e) How do other characters treat this character?

_____

Literary Devices CC1117

Characterization

Literary devices are the building blocks of storytelling. They help readers understand the meaning of a story. You will find that all stories have characters, a setting, a plot, a theme, and a point of view. In addition, many stories use flashbacks or foreshadowing to let the reader know what is happening. These are the literary devices we will study in this book.

A **character** is an imaginary person or creature in a work of fiction (play, film, or story). **Characterization** is the way the author gives his readers information about the characters. Authors use five main ways to let readers get to know characters in a story. They are: 1. the character's <u>physical appearance</u> (how the character looks); 2. the character's <u>thoughts</u> (what the character thinks); 3. the character's <u>actions</u> (what the character does); 4. the character's <u>speech</u> (what the character says); and 5. the character's <u>interactions with other characters</u> in the story (how the other characters react to him or her).

You know from your own reading that authors can create many characters that you will remember well after you've finished the stories they were in. Wilbur the Pig, Charlotte the Spider, Harry Potter, and Luke Skywalker are just a few of the most famous characters of all time. These characters are easy to remember because their authors made them seem real to their readers.

Authors create two kinds of characters. **Major characters** are well-developed. You as the reader know how they feel, think, look, and behave because the author has taken time to tell you. **Minor characters** are less developed. Readers may only know a little about them. However, minor characters are often very important to the story that is being told.

The Reading Watch Dog says,

"As you read, you will be introduced to many characters. Here are some questions to answer about each of them:"

- What is this character like?
- What does this character say?
- What does this character do?
- What does this character look like?
- Would I want to meet him or her?
- What do other characters say about him or her?

Characterization

Read the following excerpt from Charlotte's Web by E.B. White. Then, answer the questions listed below.

Charlotte's Web: Chapter One

Before Breakfast

"Where's Papa going with that ax?" said Fern to her mother as they were setting the table for breakfast.

"Out to the hoghouse," replied Mrs. Arable. "Some pigs were born last night."

"I don't see why he needs an ax," continued Fern, who was only eight.

"Well," said her mother, "one of the pigs is a runt. It's very small and weak, and it will never amount to anything. So your father has decided to do away with it."

"Do away with it?" shrieked Fern. "You mean kill it? Just because it's smaller than the others?"

Mrs. Arable put a pitcher of cream on the table. "Don't yell, Fern!" she said. "Your father is right. The pig would probably die anyway."

Fern pushed a chair out of the way and ran outdoors. The grass was wet and the earth smelled of springtime. Fern's sneakers were sopping by the time she caught up with her father.

"Please don't kill it!" she sobbed. "It's unfair."

Mr. Arable stopped walking.

"Fern," he said gently, "you will have to learn to control yourself."

"Control myself?" yelled Fern. "This is a matter of life and death, and you talk about controlling myself." Tears ran down her cheeks and she took hold of the ax and tried to pull it out of her father's hand.

"Fern," said Mr. Arable, "I know more about raising a litter of pigs than you do. A weakling makes trouble. Now run along!"

"But it's unfair," cried Fern. "The pig couldn't help being born small, could it? If I had been very small at birth, would you have killed me?"

Mr. Arable smiled. "Certainly not," he said, looking down at his daughter with love. "But this is different. A little girl is one thing, a little runty pig is another."

"I see no difference," replied Fern, still hanging on to the ax. "This is the most terrible case of injustice I ever heard of."

a) How many characters are introduced in this portion of Charlotte's Web?

_____

b) List some things you know about Fern by reading this selection.

_____

c) Who is Mrs. Arable?

_____

d) Who is Mr. Arable?

_____

e) What do you think Mr. Arable does for a living?

_____

f) What do you think "injustice" means?

_____

Using Graphic Organizers to Identify Characterization

1. **Fill in each blank with the correct term.**

graphic organizer   characterization   character
minor characters   minor character

a) A _____ is an imaginary person or creature in a work of fiction (play, film, or story).

b) _____ is the way the author gives his readers information about the characters.

c) A _____ _____ is a diagram or drawing which help you organize your ideas on paper.

d) A _____ _____ is well-developed. You as the reader know how this character feels, thinks, looks, and behaves because the author has taken time to tell you.

e) _____ _____ are less developed. You may only know a little about them.

2. **Choose one of the characters listed below and use his or her characteristics to complete the graphic organizer.**

Mickey Mouse   Garfield   Santa Claus   Sponge Bob

Character Analysis
Words
Actions
Appearance
Thoughts
Effects on Other People

Using Graphic Organizers to Identify Characterization

One important tool you can use to help you learn about the characters in the books and plays that you read is the **graphic organizer**. A **graphic organizer** is a diagram or drawing, which help you organize your ideas on paper. Graphic organizers are very handy to help you put all the elements of a character's personality into categories that are easy to remember.

There are several graphic organizers that may be of use as you study characterization. One of the most important is the **Character Chart**. The Character Chart is divided into three columns. The first column provides space for the names of the characters in the book, movie, or play. The second column asks you to list each character's relationship to the main character in the book, movie, or play. The last column asks you to list the characteristics or features of each character's personality and appearance.

Another important graphic organizer to use when you are studying characterization is the Character Study Graphic Organizer. The **Character Study Graphic Organizer** is a column of questions which ask you to tell the character's name, describe what the character is like, and list some of the words and phrases used in the book, play, or movie to tell about the character. Using the Character Study Graphic Organizer can help you remember important details about each character.

Finally, **Characterization Graphic Organizer** provides a very complete description of character traits. The Characterization Graphic Organizer is a series of six rectangles arranged like the spokes in a wheel. The rectangle in the middle is the place you will write the <u>name</u> of your character. In each rectangle that radiates from the center, one of these titles and questions are written:

1. **Dialogue** (What does the dialogue reveal about him or her?);

2. **Physical description** (What does he or she look like?);

3. **Thoughts** (What is he or she thinking?);

4. **Actions** (what do actions reveal about him or her? include gestures, motions); and

5. **Reactions of others** (What do others think of him or her?).

We will use the Characterization Graphic Organizer on the following page to analyze a particular character's traits.

Using Graphic Organizers to Identify Characterization

1. **Choose one of the characters listed in the box below or choose a character from your own reading and analyze his or her character traits using the Characterization Graphic Organizer.**

Tom Sawyer   Sleeping Beauty   The Cat in the Hat   Harry Potter
Stuart Little   Laura Ingalls
or a main character of your choice

Characterization Graphic Organizer

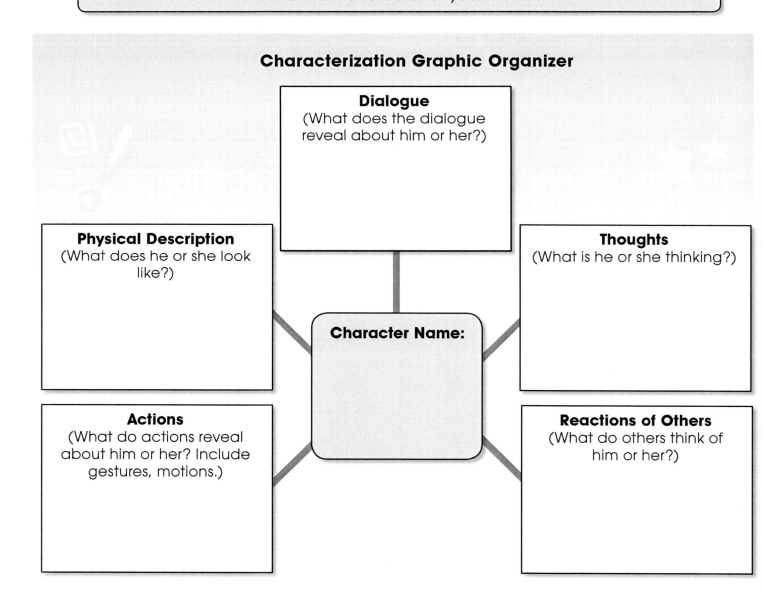

Dialogue
(What does the dialogue reveal about him or her?)

Physical Description
(What does he or she look like?)

Thoughts
(What is he or she thinking?)

Character Name:

Actions
(What do actions reveal about him or her? Include gestures, motions.)

Reactions of Others
(What do others think of him or her?)

Setting

1. **Complete each sentence with a word or phrase from the box.**

time	setting	when	place	where

The **(a)** _____ of a story is the background of the story.

It is the **(b)** _____ where the story happens and the

(c) _____ when it happens. It answers the questions of

(d) _____ and **(e)** _____.

2. **Answer each question with a complete sentence.**

a) Describe what the **setting** of a story about two ten-year-old boys might look and sound like.

_____

b) Describe the **setting** of a ghost story.

_____

c) Describe the **setting** of a story about a jungle explorer.

_____

d) Describe one of the **settings** for the fairytale, Cinderella.

_____

e) Describe the **setting** for a story about a teacher.

_____

Setting

Another important literary device is the **setting** of a story, play, or movie. The **setting** is the time and location in which a story takes place. For some stories, the setting is very important, while for others it is not.

Many times, writers will tell you more than the time and location. Sometimes, an author will describe the: a) **place** - geographical location; b) **time** - when is the story taking place? (historical period, time of day, year, etc); c) **weather conditions** - is it rainy, sunny, stormy, etc?; and d) **social conditions** - what is the daily life of the characters like?

The setting of a story can be used for other reasons, such as **to create mood or atmosphere**. "*A farm house nestled on a beautiful, grassy plain,*" paints a picture of a peaceful, happy mood, while "*a dark, ramshackle house,*" describes a scary mood.

Another use for the setting of a story is **to inform readers about different ways of life**. By providing details about clothing, customs, and speech patterns, the author gives the reader a sense of what it is really like living in that story.

Sometimes, authors use the setting **to make the action of the story seem more real**. Lifelike details can take readers to imaginary and far-away times and places.

Some writers use setting to **add to the conflict or struggle in a story**. For example, Arctic settings may include a character's struggle to survive in very cold weather.

Finally, setting may be used to **stand for some idea that the writer wants to emphasize**. For instance, a spring setting may stand for hopeful beginnings and growth, or winter may stand for death or loneliness.

The Reading Watch Dog says,
"Remember, setting provides the first bricks of the foundation on which you will build the rest of the character you are creating. No matter what else may be missing, every single story ever written since the first writer wrote the first word has taken place somewhere."

NAME: _____

Setting

1. **Circle** the word True if the statement is true. **Circle** the word False if it's false.

   a) The setting of a story, play, or movie is the time and place it happens.
   True   **False**

   b) The setting of a story is always very important to its meaning.
   True   **False**

   c) All writers tell only the time and place when they describe the settings of stories, plays or movies.
   True   **False**

   d) Setting can be used to create a mood or atmosphere for a story.
   True   **False**

   e) Informing readers about different ways of life is not a use for the setting of a story.
   True   **False**

   f) Setting can be used to make the action of the story seem more real.
   True   **False**

   g) Adding to the conflict or struggle in a story is another use for the setting of a story.
   True   **False**

2. **Complete the following exercise:**

   If I were a character in a story, here is the setting I'd use:

PLACE	WHY I CHOSE THIS PLACE
TIME	WHY I CHOSE THIS TIME

Before You Read

Using Graphic Organizers to Identify Setting

1. **Place a check mark (✔) beside the correct answer to each question.**

i)   Which of the following is not a graphic organizer?

○ **A   A chart**
○ **B   A paragraph**
○ **C   A diagram**
○ **D   A map**

ii)   Setting <u>may</u> include each of the following, <u>except</u>:

○ **A   Time**
○ **B   Place**
○ **C   Date**
○ **D   Characters**

2. **Choose one of the following fairy tales from the box, and use its setting to complete the graphic organizer below.**

> Little Red Riding Hood   Snow White and the Seven Dwarfs   Hansel and Gretel
> Goldilocks and the Three Bears   The Three Little Pigs   Jack and the Beanstalk

Meaning of Setting Map

Where does the story take place?	When does the story take place?	Changes in the setting during the story:
DETAILS!	DETAILS!	DETAILS!

Using Graphic Organizers to Identify Setting

The setting of a story is created by a writer's use of words. The amount of details included is left entirely up to him or her. Many authors choose to let their readers come up with some of the details of the setting on their own. They must then use clues to guess the time and place.

Graphic organizers are charts or drawings that can help you put all the elements of a story's setting into categories that are easy to remember. There are many graphic organizers that may be helpful to you as you study setting. The three most helpful are the **Analyzing the Setting in a Story Chart**, the **Three Elements of Setting Graphic Organizer**, and the **Meaning of Setting Map**.

The **Analyzing the Setting in a Story Chart** asks you to answer questions about the setting of a particular story, play, or movie. It is presented in a two-columned chart with the heading of the first column labeled, "Questions to Ask about Setting," and the second column labeled, "Responses from the Story." This graphic organizer asks questions such as: "What does the setting tell us about the characters?," and "How would you describe the atmosphere or mood created by the setting?" We will work with this graphic organizer on the following page.

The **Three Elements of Setting Graphic Organizer** is a setting map showing three rectangles labeled, "Place," "Time," and "Environment," merging together to make the literary device, "Setting." This graphic organizer also includes some tips for developing the setting of a story.

The last graphic organizer to use for setting is the **Meaning of Setting Map**. It is a three-columned chart with the headings, "Where does the story take place?," "When does the story take place?," and "Changes in the setting during the story." Underneath each heading is a space for details. You will find that using graphic organizers as you study the literary device of setting will be very helpful.

The Reading Watch Dog says,

"Keys to a story's setting"

- date • location
- weather • scenery
- rooms • clothing
- local customs • dialects

Using Graphic Organizers to Identify Setting

1. **Complete this graphic organizer using information from a book that you have read in the past.**

ANALYZING SETTING IN A STORY

Title of Book: _____

Author: _____

QUESTIONS TO ASK ABOUT SETTING	RESPONSES FROM THE STORY
1. What is the setting? Historical period? Country or locale? Season of the year? Weather? Time of day? What are the sights? Sounds? Tastes? Smells? What other details establish a sense of place?	
2. Are the characters in conflict with the setting? What do the characters want? Does the setting keep them from getting what they want?	
3. What does the setting tell us about the characters? What feelings or attitudes do the characters reveal toward the setting? Fear? Pleasure? Challenge? Dislike? Respect? Other feelings or attitudes?	
4. How would you describe the atmosphere or mood created by the setting? Is it gloomy? Cheerful? Mysterious? Threatening? Other descriptions?	

Plot

1.   Match the meaning on the right with its term on the left.

A	plot		describes the characters and the setting of the story.	**1**
B	narrative		a tying-up of all the loose ends left in the story.	**2**
C	introduction		refers to what happens and how it happens in a story, play, or movie.	**3**
D	rising action		the section of the plot when readers find out more about the main characters and conflicts are introduced.	**4**
E	climax		any written work that tells a story, such as a short story, a novel, or a play.	**5**
F	falling action		the "high point" of a story, when the major conflicts end up in some kind of final showdown.	**6**
G	resolution		a time immediately following the climax.	**7**

2.   Choose one of the fairy tales in the box below and write a summary of its plot.

> Little Red Riding Hood   Snow White and the Seven Dwarfs   Hansel and Gretel
> Goldilocks and the Three Bears   The Three Little Pigs   Jack and the Beanstalk

_____

_____

_____

_____

_____

_____

Plot

Now it is time to discuss another very important literary device, **plot**. **Plot** refers to what happens and how it happens in a narrative. A **narrative** is any written work that tells a story, such as a short story, a novel, or a play. **Plot** can also be defined as a "plan of action for a story, play, or movie." Plot is usually the most important element in a story.

The plot of a story usually unfolds in a particular way. The **introduction** or **opening** describes the characters and the setting of the story. Next, the **rising action** happens. It is during this section of the plot that conflicts are introduced, and readers find out more about the main characters in the story. The third part of a plot is called the **climax**. The climax is the "high point" of a story, when the major conflicts end up in some kind of final showdown (a fight, an argument, physical action, or a very tense emotional moment). The climax is the point in the story where something CHANGES. Then, comes the **falling action**, a time immediately following the climax. The falling action deals with the results of the climax. Finally, the plot ends in a **resolution**, or a tying-up of all the loose ends left in the story. Most resolutions leave the readers with a sense of closure or completion. The five stages of plot development are illustrated in the diagram below.

The Reading Watch Dog says,

"Here is a Plot Diagram to help you understand the plot sequence of a story:"

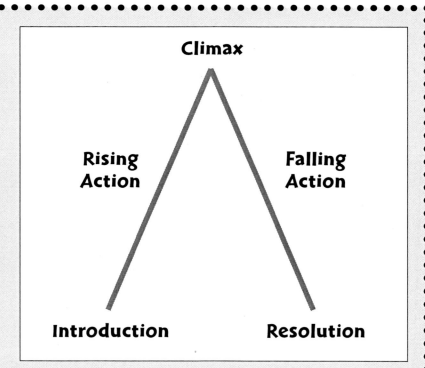

Climax

Rising Action

Falling Action

Introduction

Resolution

NAME: _____

Plot

1. **Circle** **the word or phrase that correctly completes each statement.**

a) _____ refers to what happens and how it happens in a narrative.

    i) setting   **ii) plot**   **iii) characterization.**

b) A _____ is any written work that tells a story, such as a short story, a novel, or a play.

    i) science book   **ii) narrative**   **iii) math book**

c) The _____ describes the characters and the setting of the story.

    i) rising action   **ii) climax**   **iii) introduction**

d) The _____ is during the section of the plot where conflicts are introduced and that readers find out more about the main characters in the story.

    i) rising action   **ii) climax**   **iii) introduction**

e) The _____ is the "high point" of a story, when the major conflicts end up in some kind of final showdown.

    i) rising action   **ii) climax**   **iii) introduction**

f) The _____ deals with the results of the climax.

    i) resolution   **ii) introduction**   **iii) falling action**

g) A plot ends in a _____, or a tying-up of all the loose ends left in the story.

    i) resolution   **ii) introduction**   **iii) falling action**

h) There are _____ stages of plot development.

    i) five   **ii) three**   **iii) seven**

2. **Label the following plot diagram.**

c)

b)

d)

a)

e)

     Literary Devices CC1117

Using Graphic Organizers to Identify Plot

1. Circle the word True if the statement is true. Circle the word False if it's false.

a) The characters and setting of a story are described in the climax.

    True   **False**

b) The things that happen and how they happen in a narrative are called its resolution.

    True   **False**

c) In the rising action of a story's plot, readers find out the conflicts and more about the main characters in the story.

    True   **False**

d) Plot can also be defined as a "plan of action for a story, play, or movie.

    True   **False**

e) The time immediately after the climax is called the falling action.

    True   **False**

f) Conflict is the struggle between the opposing forces in a story.

    True   **False**

2. **Answer each question with a complete sentence.**

a) What is a graphic organizer?

_____

_____

b) Why would a writer use a graphic organizer?

_____

_____

c) Suppose you were writing a story and had only paper and pencil at your desk. Could you use a graphic organizer if your teacher had not printed one for you? What could you do to get a graphic organizer to use?

_____

_____

_____

Using Graphic Organizers to Identify Plot

Graphic organizers are charts or drawings that can help you put your ideas in some kind of order. When you use a graphic organizer in plot development, its main purpose is to help you place the stages of the plot in the order that they happened in the story. There are several good graphic organizers to use for this purpose.

Another part of plot development that you will need to know, is the kind of conflict that exists in a story. **Conflict** is the **struggle between the opposing forces in a story**. The action in the story depends on this conflict. There are **four basic forms of conflict**: 1) character against character, 2) character against self, 3) character against nature, and 4) character against society. Your teacher may ask you to tell which kind(s) of conflict(s) exist in the story you are reading.

One very good graphic organizer to use in plot development is the **Five Stages of Plot Development in a Story, Movie, or Play**. The organizer is a large circle that has been divided into five parts. It looks like a pie that has been sliced into five pieces. Beginning at the top of the circle and continuing clockwise, each part is numbered and has a fill-out line with a description of a particular stage of plot development in parentheses. The numbers show what happens first in the plot of a story, what happens second, and so forth. Your job is to put the name of each stage on the correct line.

Another graphic organizer to use for plot development is the **Conflict Type Chart**. This chart is made up of four columns labeled "character against character," "character against self," "character against nature," and "character against society." To complete this organizer, use a book, play, or movie that you've read or seen and identify the type(s) of conflict(s) that take place in it.

The last graphic organizer to use for plot development is the **Conflict Map**. It is a chart with three columns. The first column's heading is "What is the Conflict?" The second heading is "Why Does this Conflict Occur?," and the third heading is "What are some ways the conflict could be resolved?" Completing this map will help you understand the types of conflicts that are in the stories you read.

The Reading Watch Dog says,
"Graphic organizers are key writing tools. Unlike many others that just have one purpose, graphic organizers are flexible and can be used for many different purposes."

Using Graphic Organizers to Identify Plot

1. **Choose one of the following fairy tales from the box or choose one of your own and use the elements of its plot to complete the graphic organizer below.**

> *Little Red Riding Hood   Snow White and the Seven Dwarfs   Hansel and Gretel*
> *Goldilocks and the Three Bears   The Three Little Pigs   Jack and the Beanstalk*

The Five Stages of Plot Development in a Story, Play, or Movie

a) _____
(Describes the characters and the setting of the story.)

e) _____
(A tying-up of all the loose ends left in the story.)

b) _____
(Conflicts are introduced, and readers find out more about the characters.)

d) _____
(Deals with the results of the climax.)

c) _____
(The "high point" of a story.)

Theme

1. **Complete each statement with a word or phrase from the box.**

Aesop's Fables	setting	character	theme	literary devices	plot

a) _____ _____ are the building blocks of storytelling.

b) An imaginary person or creature in a work of fiction (play, film, or story) is a

_____.

c) The time and location in which a story takes place is its _____.

d) _____ _____ are a collection of short stories that teach a life lesson or moral.

e) The _____ of any story is the main idea or point that the author is trying to tell the audience.

f) _____ refers to what happens and how it happens in a narrative.

2. **Match the title of each fairy tale with its major theme by placing the correct letter in the blank before its matching theme. More than one fairy tale may have the same theme.**

A) Cinderella	B) Snow White	C) Hansel and Gretel
D) The Three Little Pigs	E) Sleeping Beauty	F) Jack and the Beanstalk

i) [ ] One character is jealous of another character's beauty and goodness.

ii) [ ] Characters are put to a test.

iii) [ ] Foolishness or evil is punished.

iv) [ ] Characters get help from a magical creature.

v) [ ] Characters marry royalty.

vi) [ ] Honesty and cleverness are rewarded.

Theme

All narrative stories, plays, or movies have a literary device called, "**theme**." The **theme** of any story is the main idea or point that the author is trying to tell the audience. The theme is also what the author wants you to remember most about the story. Sometimes, the theme of a story is the answer to the question, "*What did you learn from reading this?*"

The Reading Watch Dog says,

"Here are some Key Themes in stories, plays, and movies:"

- Things are not always as they appear to be.
- Love is blind.
- Believe in yourself.
- People are afraid of change.
- Don't judge a book by its cover.

It is important to remember that the **theme** of a story is not the same thing as the *subject* of a story. The **theme** refers to the entire message that the writer is trying to send with his story through the use of characterization, action, and images. The subject of a story is simply its main idea, or the topic the story is about.

An author can express the theme(s) of a story in four ways: 1) by the feelings of the main characters, 2) through the thoughts of the main characters, 3) through events of the story, and 4) through the actions of the characters.

A good place to start when learning how to identify theme, is to look at **Aesop's Fables**. These are short tales that were written long ago for the purpose of teaching morals or lessons about life. In these tales, you can identify the theme of the story right away, because the author gives it to you with the tale.

On the following page, you will find an example of one of **Aesop's Fables** called, "*The Ant and the Grasshopper.*" Read the fable and see if you can guess the moral or theme that it is trying to communicate to you.

Theme

1. **Answer each question with a short paragraph.**

    a) Explain the difference between the **theme** and **subject** of a story, play, or movie.

_____

_____

    b) Discuss the four ways that most authors express the theme of their narrative works.

_____

_____

_____

2. **Read the following fable, "The Ant and the Grasshopper," and then answer the questions.**

> In a field one summer's day a Grasshopper was hopping about, chirping and singing to its heart's content. An Ant passed by, wearily pushing a piece of corn he was taking to the nest.
>
> "Why not come and play with me," said the Grasshopper, "instead of working so hard?"
>
> "I am helping to put up food for the winter," said the Ant, "and I think that you should do the same thing."
>
> "Why worry about winter?" said the Grasshopper; "we have got plenty of food right now." But the Ant went on its way and continued its working. When the winter came the Grasshopper had no food, and found itself dying of hunger, while it saw the ants distributing corn and grain every day from the stores they had collected in the summer.

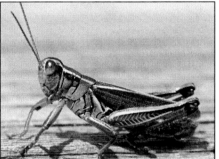

    a) Which best states the theme of "The Ant and the Grasshopper?"

        i) **"Pretty is as pretty does."**

        ii) **"Saving today will help you tomorrow."**

       iii) **"Never do today what you can put off until tomorrow."**

    b) List the characters in "The Ant and the Grasshopper."

_____

📝 *Before You Read*

Using Graphic Organizers to Identify Theme

1. **(Circle)** the word True if the statement is true. **(Circle)** the word False if it's false.

   a) Graphic organizers are communication devices.

       True   **False**

   b) Graphic organizers do not show the relationships between two or more concepts.

       True   **False**

   c) Another name for a learning strategy is "tool for learning."

       True   **False**

   d) There are no graphic organizers that make a story's theme easier to understand.

       True   **False**

2. **Listed below are some common themes in young readers' books, movies, and plays. On the line next to each theme, write at least one story title with that particular theme.**

   Believe in Yourself _____

   Accepting Others' Differences _____

   Overcoming Challenges _____

   Don't Be Afraid to Try New Things _____

   Teamwork _____

   Honesty _____

   Always Be Kind to Others _____

   Be Happy with What You Have _____

Using Graphic Organizers to Identify Theme

Graphic organizers are **communication devices**. They show the **structure** or make-up of concepts as well as the **relationships** between concepts. By presenting information visually, graphic organizers make it easier for you to understand complex material. Another good reason to use graphic organizers is that they help you separate more important information from the less important. Finally, using graphic organizers gives you more **strategies** or tools for learning.

The **Theme Tree** graphic organizer is very helpful when you are asked to identify the main theme and the parts of the story which relate to it. The **Theme Tree** is a line drawing of a big, leafless tree with several branches. Write the main theme on the trunk of the tree, then write each part of the story that relates to the theme on the individual branches.

The **Theme(s) Comparison Chart** is another good graphic organizer to use when you identify theme. The chart is made up of four boxes arranged with one box labeled, "Theme" on the first line. The next line has two boxes side-by-side labeled, "Differences," and "Similarities." On the third line there is one box labeled, "Conclusions." Identify the main theme(s) of the story on the first line, then write the differences between the themes in the boxes on the second line. Finally, you should write your conclusions about the themes in the box labeled "Conclusions."

The **Theme Chart** is an excellent organizer to use when you wish to discuss the major parts of the theme's development. List the *title* of your book, play, or movie on the first line of the **Theme Chart**. Next, list the *main characters* in the story. Third, you should identify the *major conflict(s)* or the *struggle(s)* between the opposing forces in a story. Next, list the *main theme* of the story, then identify the *Beginning of the Theme*, the *Development of the Theme*, the *Climax of the Theme*, and the *Resolution of the Theme*. All three of these organizers will help you understand the theme of a story.

NAME: _____

Using Graphic Organizers to Identify Theme

1. Choose a book, movie, or play that you have read recently. Put its title on the first line and complete the graphic organizer using information about its characters and theme.

Theme Chart

Title	
Main Characters	
Main Conflict	
Main Theme	
Beginning of Theme	
Development of Theme	
Climax of Theme	
Resolution of Theme	

NAME: _____

Point of View

1. **Match the meaning on the right with its term on the left.**

A | point of view of a story | : : : : : : | I, me and we. | **1**
B | first person point of view | : : : : : : | his own opinions, thoughts, and ideas. | **2**
C | third person point of view | : : : : : : | a character in the story is the narrator. | **3**
D | first person pronouns | : : : : : : | the way a story gets told and who tells it. | **4**
E | third person pronouns | : : : : : : | he, she, and they. | **5**
F | storyteller's point of view | : : : : : : | the story is being told by an outside observer (someone who is not in the story). | **6**

2. **The following are parts of stories written by students. Below each part, (circle) its point of view.**

a) The first time Carlos saw the Martian, he thought it was the oddest looking creature he'd ever seen. However, the Martian thought Carlos was pretty funny looking, too.

     First Person Point of View   Third Person Point of View

b) I pressed the large yellow button, and the spaceship started to rumble. Kristy looked at me and asked, "What are you doing?" I told her that I had no earthly idea what I was doing.

     First Person Point of View   Third Person Point of View

c) When my brother got home, I was afraid to tell him that I'd peeked at his science fair project. But I knew I had to tell my brother. After all, the machine had made my left hand disappear!

     First Person Point of View   Third Person Point of View

d) The astronauts wandered farther and farther away from their ship. Finally, they looked up and saw that this planet's moon was purple.

     First Person Point of View   Third Person Point of View

Point of View

Every book, movie, poem, and play that tells a story contains a literary device called **point of view**. The **point of view** is **the way a story gets told and who tells it**. When a writer begins a narrative or story, he or she must decide who will tell it. The majority of the time, storytelling is done by using a **first person point of view** or a **third person point of view**. We will discuss other types of **point of view** at a later time.

The Reading Watch Dog says,
"Here are some Keys to Understanding Point of View:"

First person point of view

A character in the story is the narrator. This character is telling the story. The narrator uses the pronouns **I, me, and we**.

In **first-person point of view**, readers learn about events at the same time **as the narrator learns about them.**

Examples of First Person Point of View:

"I walked home from school today with **my** friends. **We** stopped for ice cream. **I** had vanilla. It's **my** favorite."

"When **I** got up this morning **I** brushed **my** teeth. Then **I** got dressed and ate **my** breakfast."

Third person point of view

The story is being told by an **outside observer** (someone who is not in the story). The author uses the pronouns **he, she, and they**.

In **third-person point of view, the outside observer tells about the thoughts, actions, and feelings of the other characters.**

Examples of Third Person Point of View:

Ted plays on a baseball team. **He** loves to play with **his** team. **He** has a game next week. **His** coach thinks **he's** a good baseball player.

The princess was locked in the tower. **She** had no way to escape. **She** hoped that a prince would rescue **her**. **Her** wish came true. He came and took **her** to his castle.

Generally, authors write books, plays, or movies **to entertain, persuade, or inform** his or her **audience**. This means that an author uses the storyteller's **point of view** to express his own opinions, thoughts, and ideas.

Remember, **someone is always between the reader and the action of the story**. That someone is telling the story from his or her own **point of view**. The **point of view** from which the people, events, and details of a story are seen is important to understand when you read a story. The tone and feel of the story, and even its meaning, can change depending on who is telling it.

NAME: _____

Point of View

1. **Circle** the word or phrase that correctly completes each statement.

   a) When an author expresses his or her feelings, opinions, thoughts and ideas it is called _____.

       i) entertainment   **ii) point of view**   **iii) climax**

   b) The following are three main reasons why an author writes a story, EXCEPT to _____.

       i) inform   **ii) persuade**   **iii) entertain**   **iv) make sure the reader likes the story**

   c) The way a story gets told and who tells it is called its _____.

       i) point of view   **ii) setting**   **iii) characterization**

   d) The person who is telling a story is called the _____.

       i) talker   **ii) listener**   **iii) narrator**

2. The fairy tale, "The Three Little Pigs," is written in third person point of view. Use the lines below to rewrite the story from **the wolf's point of view** (first person). If you need a refresher of the story, go to http://216.36.206.143/Three_Little_Pigs/storybook/storybook.htm on your classroom computer.

_____

_____

_____

_____

_____

_____

_____

_____

_____

_____

_____

Using Graphic Organizers to Identify Point of View

1. **Circle** the word True if the statement is true. **Circle** the word False if it's false.

a) Graphic organizers give students visual pictures of how concepts fit together.

True   **False**

b) Every graphic organizer must be complicated to be useful.

True   **False**

c) Graphic organizers can be used in other subjects besides language arts.

True   **False**

d) A writer must decide his or her point of view before beginning to write a story.

True   **False**

e) All writers use the same point of view when they write.

True   **False**

f) There are only two points of view.

True   **False**

2. **Read the following poem by Karma Wilson and then answer the questions.**

What Your Cat Might Be Thinking
I'm the center of the universe.
I'm all-out royalty.
There really isn't anyone
who's near as good as me.
And everything that's ever done
is done just for my bidding.
And I shall banish anyone

I do not deem befitting.
Laps were made to be my throne,
and hands were made to pet me.
And anything I want to do,
of course, you have to let me.
And if you open up a book,
then that's to lay my head on.
And if you put your sweater down,

well, that's for me to shed on.
And if you plant a pretty plant,
well, that's for me to chew.
And if you bring a puppy home,
well, that's the end of you.

(McElderry Books, 2009)

a) What is the title of this poem? _____

b) From whose point of view is this poem told? _____

c) Is this first person or third person point of view? _____

d) How do you know? _____

Using Graphic Organizers to Identify Point of View

You have learned that the **point of view** of a book, movie, or play is **the way a story gets told and who tells it**. One of the first tasks a writer has to achieve after deciding to tell a story, is how information about the characters and plot will be told to the readers. Although there are others, the two most often used points of view are the **first person** and the **third person** points of view.

    Point of view is often shortened to the letters POV. In your reading, you may see these letters used to stand for point of view. Point of view is the way a writer communicates his or her purpose(s) or reasons for writing. The three most common purposes for writing a story are to entertain, to inform, or to persuade.

You have also learned that **graphic organizers** are used to show the elements, or parts of a story, and how they fit together. Using a graphic organizer helps you visualize or see the process of story writing.

There are two good graphic organizers that will help you understand point of view. The first one is called the **Character's Point of View Map**. This graphic organizer is a series of five boxes that are arranged on top of each other. Write the title of the story, play, or movie that you are discussing in the first box. In the next box, write the name of the character from whose point of view the story is told, and whether this point of view is in the first or third person. In the next three boxes, give examples from the story that show the type of point of view the character has.

The second graphic organizer to use is called the **Literary Point of View Spider**. This organizer is a diagram that resembles a spider, with place for the character's name and point of view on the body. Each of the "legs" of the spider is a place to write examples of the author's opinions, ideas, and thoughts that make up his or her point of view. We will use a **Literary Point of View Spider** on the following page.

Using Graphic Organizers to Identify Point of View

1. **Read the following poem, "Thanksgiving from the Turkey's Point of View," and then complete the graphic organizer.**

Thanksgiving from the Turkey's Point of View

Thank Goodness! It's finally over -
And now I'll get some rest...
It's been two weeks since I have dared
To go back to the nest.
I trust my mate is still around...
My lovely hen, dear Mabel -
I hope she wasn't dumb enough
To grace some human's table.
I'll never know why human folk
Think it's so much fun
To hit the woods and murder -
We turkeys with those guns

I'm six years old, last hatching -
And friend that's quite a feat...
With open season on us birds...
When we become...just MEAT!
I'll strut my stuff, and gobble loud
For just awhile...again!
I'll hide deep in the forest...
For it's Christmas coming then!
So why did I hen-scratch this out?
And post it here for you?
That you might see Thanksgiving
From the turkey's point of view.
http://poetry-magazine.com/poetry/poetry-006/03page.htm#Turkey

LITERARY POINT OF VIEW

Examples of the Author's Opinions, Ideas, and Thoughts

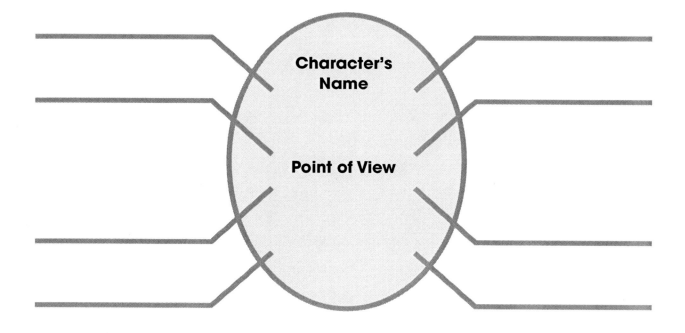

Character's Name

Point of View

Before You Read

Foreshadowing & Flashback

1. **Circle** **the word or phrase that correctly completes each statement.**

a) _____ happens when an author mentions or hints at something that will happen later in the story.

    i) flashback   **ii) foreshadowing**   **iii) fortune telling**

b) _____ occur when an author refers back to an event that has already taken place in the story.

    i) flashbacks   **ii) foreshadowing**   **iii) climaxes**

c) _____ often serves two purposes.

    i) a flashbacks   **ii) foreshadowing**   **iii) a literary device**

2. Identify each passage as **foreshadowing** or a **flashback** by circling the correct term.

a) The school day began just like every other school day. Little did Mrs. Jones know that this would be her last day at school for a long while.

    i) foreshadowing   **ii) flashback**

b) As he worked, Jim thought back to the time he helped his father paint the house.

    i) foreshadowing   **ii) flashback**

c) When Julie saw that Ben had brought a knife to school, she knew that nothing good would come of it.

    i) foreshadowing   **ii) flashback**

d) Kate's grandmother said, "That's nothing! When I was a little girl, I walked seven miles to school each day!"

    i) foreshadowing   **ii) flashback**

e) Her fairy godmother told Cinderella that going to the ball might change her life.

    i) foreshadowing   **ii) flashback**

Foreshadowing & Flashback

As you learn more about literary devices, you will become familiar with the terms, **foreshadowing** and **flashbacks**. Both elements are important because they can add depth to the characters in a story or suspense to its plot.

Foreshadowing happens when an author mentions or hints at something that will happen later in the story. Here is a pointer that may help you remember the definition of **foreshadowing**. Try breaking the word "foreshadowing" into two parts. "Fore" means "ahead," and a "shadow" is a glimpse of something without seeing its complete details. An example of foreshadowing occurs in *A Christmas Carol* by Charles Dickens when the Ghost of Christmas Yet to Come shows Ebenezer Scrooge how things might be at his death.

Foreshadowing often serves two purposes. It builds suspense by raising questions that make the reader want to go on and find out more about the event that is being foreshadowed. Foreshadowing is also a way of making a story more believable by preparing the reader for events that will soon happen.

Flashbacks occur when an author refers back to an event that has already taken place in the story. Flashbacks give us the ability to see into a character's past in real time. They interrupt the current action of a story to show a scene from the past. Again, using A Christmas Carol, we can see that a flashback happens when the Ghost of Christmas Past visits Scrooge and takes him back to the time when he was a young man.

The Reading Watch Dog says,
"The key reasons an author uses foreshadowing is to make readers wonder what will happen in the remainder of the book. Flashbacks can appear as a character's memories or dreams, or can be included in the narrations of the story. Flashbacks allow readers to learn background information that is key to understanding the rest of the story."

NAME: _____

Foreshadowing & Flashback

1. **Answer the following questions using complete sentences.**

a) What is **foreshadowing**?

_____

_____

_____

b) What are the **two purposes** that foreshadowing serves?

_____

_____

c) What is a **flashback**?

_____

_____

2. **Read the following excerpts from "Little Red Riding Hood" and tell whether the underlined portion in each one is an example of a flashback or foreshadowing.**

Once upon a time, there was a little girl who lived with her mother. Her mother asked her to take her old and lonely grandmother some food one day. "<u>Don't stop along the way. Go straight to your Grandma's house and back. Don't talk to any strangers and watch out for the wolf in the woods! Now get along!</u>"

a) **flashback** or **foreshadowing?** (Circle the correct choice)

The wolf went up to Little Red Riding Hood and told her that he knew a shortcut. <u>Little Red Riding Hood thought back to what her mother told her. "Don't talk to any strangers and watch out for the wolf in the woods!"</u> But it was too late, she had already listened to the wolf's directions.

b) **flashback** or **foreshadowing?** (Circle the correct choice)

Literary Devices CC1117

Irony and Symbolism

1. Put the letter of the meaning next to the correct term.

A	irony	⋮	when a person <u>says</u> one thing and means another.	**1**
B	literary symbolism	⋮	when a set of circumstances or a result is the opposite of what might be expected.	**2**
C	symbol	⋮	an expression in which the intended meaning of the words is the direct opposite of their usual sense.	**3**
D	verbal irony	⋮	when an object in a story, play, or movie stands for a feeling, idea, or concept.	**4**
E	situational irony	⋮	objects that stand for or represent other things or ideas.	**5**

2. Tell whether the following examples of *irony* are situational or verbal by (circling) the correct term.

a) A little girl names her white cat "Midnight".

Verbal irony   **Situational irony**

b) The son of the police chief is arrested for burglary.

Verbal irony   **Situational irony**

c) It is a dark, gloomy, rainy, day and someone says, "Wow, what a gorgeous day!"

Verbal irony   **Situational irony**

3. Sketch a symbol for each of the following qualities.

a) Fear

b) Happiness

Irony and Symbolism

Irony and **symbolism** are two other literary devices that can make a story, play, or movie more interesting and meaningful. Both are used very often in children's literature.

Irony is an expression in which the intended meaning of the words is the direct opposite of their usual sense. In other words, a phrase or sentence becomes **ironic** when a person says one thing and means another such as: "Tessa called Jim's *stupid* plan '*very clever*.'" Using words to be ironic is called **verbal irony**.

Another type of **irony** occurs when a set of circumstances or a result is the opposite of what might be expected. For example, it is **ironic** (and tragic) when a rescue helicopter crashes. This type of irony is called **situational irony**.

Literary symbolism happens when an object in a story, play, or movie symbolizes or stands for a feeling, idea, or concept. We see examples of **symbolism** everywhere in our daily life. A cross standing for a place of worship, an American flag symbolizing the United States, and a heart suggesting true love are all examples of **symbolism**.

Writers often use **symbolism** in their stories. Fairy tales, especially, are filled with symbols. The big, bad wolf stands for danger and evil, the king symbolizes the highest authority, and a beautiful red rose means true love. Try to think of other symbols in your favorite fairy and folk tales. You might be surprised at how many you come up with!

The Reading Watch Dog says,

"Tips to Understanding Irony and Symbolism"

• Irony is when what we say or write conveys the opposite of its literal meaning. For example, "Mother will be happy to hear what you have done now," when you know that Mother will not be at all happy. Other examples: "Nice weather!" on a rainy day, or "Of course I believe you," in a sarcastic manner.

• A symbol is something that represents something else, either by association or in appearance. It can be a material object or a written sign used to represent something invisible. For example, a skull and crossbones stands for 'Poison' and a gold coin means 'riches.'

Irony and Symbolism

Place a check mark (✔) beside the best answer to each question.

1. Which of the following is an example of **situational** irony?

    ○ **A** The rabbit ran away from the boy.
    ○ **B** She told everyone what a dreary day it was.
    ○ **C** A carpenter's roof caves in.
    ○ **D** Sally is beautiful.

2. Which of the following is an example of **verbal** irony?

    ○ **A** A right handed person is called "Righty"
    ○ **B** A tall boy is called "Shorty"
    ○ **C** A smart robber gets caught.
    ○ **D** A best selling actor's latest movie loses money at the box office.

3. The student with the highest grades in cooking class makes a terrible dessert. This is an example of:

    ○ **A** Verbal irony
    ○ **B** Situational irony
    ○ **C** Literary symbolism

4. When a narrator or a character in a book, play, or movie says one thing and means another, it is an example of:

    ○ **A** Verbal irony
    ○ **B** Situational irony
    ○ **C** Literary symbolism

5. When an object in a story, play, or movie stands for a feeling, idea, or concept, it is an example of:

    ○ **A** Verbal irony
    ○ **B** Situational irony
    ○ **C** Literary symbolism

(Characterization) *On another sheet of paper, write down the names of two of your favorite characters you have encountered in books you have read. Make a list of specific reasons why you chose these characters as "favorites." Make a list of what you remember about how the author developed each of the two characters.*

When you complete the above activities, list the ways the author makes the characters come to life, including each character's:

- physical characteristics (or lack thereof),
- interaction with other characters,
- interaction with his or her environment,
- thoughts and/or outlook on life,
- revelations about his or her past, and
- dialect or way of speaking.

- -

📝 Writing Task # 2

(Writing a Character Sketch) *Write a character sketch about somebody you know well — for example, a parent, best friend, relative, or neighbor. A character sketch highlights several important characteristics or personality traits of a person — a real person, a person in literature, or an imagined person. A good character sketch provides support detail for each identified trait.*

Below is a sample character sketch for you to read. Try to tell about the good qualities your character has. Be sure to use complete sentences and correct paragraph form.

My friend Liz is a true best friend. She always supports me in everything I want to do. When I wanted to go up North, she said she thought it would be a great experience and that it would help me develop my sense of adventure.

Liz is not only a great supporter. She also trusts me to give her my honest opinion and to say what I feel. When she was upset with her sister one time, she asked what I thought about it and I said she should wait and then she would find out the real reason why her sister was mad at her. And it happened that way. She knew she could trust me.

Liz can be a barrel of fun when she is in the mood. I really like when she does silly things. One night, we rented three movies and watched all three while we ate popcorn, cheese and crackers, and a whole box of chocolates. We gabbed about everything and even imagined what it would be like to live like some of the characters in the movies.

Since my best friend is now living over 500 miles away, I miss all the laughter she brought to my life and the times I could ask her opinion on things that troubled me. But I can still hear the sound of her voice and ask her opinion on the telephone!

Writing Task #3

(Setting – A Childhood Place or Event) *Think of an important place or event from your childhood. On another sheet of paper, write a fictionalized children's story about a child who goes to this place or this event for someone about the same age that you were when the place or event occured. Because you're writing a fictionalized record of the place or event, your details don't have to conform to actual truth. You can weave two or three (or more) memories about the place together in one story. You can make up things about the place that you're not sure of or that you wish had occurred. Your story should show how you thought and felt about the place or event as a child. Your reader has never been to the place you are describing, so you will need to use specific, concrete details which make the place vivid and your perspectives clear.*

_____

_____

_____

_____

_____

Writing Task #4

(Plot) *Remember that the plot of a story refers to what happens and how it happens in a narrative. Sometimes, a photo can make you wonder what happened and how it happened.*

Look at the photo below and then write a short story about the characters pictured in it.

Jessica Wanstall, an 11-year-old girl standing 4'10," caught a record-size catfish.
Photo: BNPS Pictures http://www.parentdish.com/category/weird-but-true

(Theme) *The theme of any story is the main idea or point that the author is trying to tell the audience. The theme is also what the author wants you to remember most about the story. Some themes can be expressed in only one or two words. Below you will find a list of several common literary themes.*

Choose one theme and on your own paper, write at least a five paragraph story about it.

Literary Themes

- Ambition • Beauty • Betrayal • Courage • Duty • Fear

- Freedom • Happiness • Jealousy • Loneliness • Love • Loyalty

- Perseverance • Prejudice • Suffering • Truth

- -

■ Writing Task # 6

(Flashbacks) *Many movies use the literary device, flashback, to tell their stories. Think of a movie you have seen in which the main character(s) flashback to something that has happened in the past.*
Now, write about this movie and the flashback(s) it included.

_____

_____

_____

_____

_____

_____

_____

Crossword

Word List
action	elements	irony
Aesops	falling	plot
character	flashback	setting
climax	graphic	situation
	introduction	view

Across

1. A person in a story.
5. Point of _____.
6. The time and location of a story.
9. Plan of action for a story.
10. _____ action.
12. The first stage of plot development.
13. _____ organizer.
14. _____ fables.

Down

2. Rising _____.
3. Literary _____.
4. The "high point" of a story.
7. _____ irony.
8. Refers back to an event that has already happened.
11. An expression in which the meaning of the words are the opposite of their usual meaning.

After You Read

Word Search

Find the following key words from the reading. The words are written horizontally, vertically, diagonally and some are even backwards.

characters	flashbacks	plot	symbolism
climax	foreshadowing	point of view	theme
conflict	irony	resolution	
fables	literary elements	rising action	
falling action	narrative	setting	

f	o	r	e	s	h	a	d	o	w	i	n	g	n	m	l
s	t	e	z	u	q	i	b	j	d	s	l	r	e	i	s
m	l	s	y	m	b	o	l	i	s	m	o	p	t	s	f
n	p	o	i	n	t	o	f	v	i	e	w	e	x	e	a
o	i	l	r	g	l	c	b	c	g	b	r	o	q	t	l
i	e	u	u	e	k	v	o	d	s	a	p	s	u	t	l
t	d	t	o	f	j	n	p	r	r	s	r	r	m	i	i
c	a	i	d	o	f	l	o	y	r	s	o	e	r	n	n
a	u	o	g	l	h	l	e	s	e	u	e	t	t	g	g
g	o	n	i	y	f	l	a	s	h	b	a	c	k	s	a
n	r	c	n	p	e	k	p	e	e	d	j	a	f	i	c
i	t	o	t	m	e	a	l	d	i	m	h	r	h	u	t
s	r	f	e	h	u	g	o	a	r	t	e	a	d	q	i
i	r	n	a	r	r	a	t	i	v	e	s	h	t	h	o
r	t	c	z	d	y	c	x	a	m	i	l	c	t	m	n
s	k	h	o	l	s	e	l	b	a	f	o	h	j	o	l

Literary Devices CC1117

Comprehension Quiz

22

Put a "T" in front of each true statement and put an "F" in front of each false statement.

1. Literary devices help readers understand the meaning of a story.

2. A character is a simple line drawing of a person.

3. In a book, play, or movie, major characters are well-developed and minor characters are less developed.

4. A crossword puzzle is a diagram or drawing which help you organize your ideas on paper.

5. Character Analysis Graphic Organizer asks the writer to describe the main character's words, actions, appearance, thoughts, and effect on other people.

6. The setting of a story is the time and location in which it takes place.

7. The setting of a story is never used to create mood or atmosphere.

8. Weather, scenery, rooms, local customs, clothing, and dialects are keys to a story's setting.

9. Characters are usually the most important elements in a story.

10. Plot refers to what happens and how it happens in a narrative.

10

Write the answers to the following questions.

11. Draw a plot diagram. Be sure to include all five of the stages of plot development.

2

12. What is the climax of a story, play, or movie?

_____

_____

_____

2

SUBTOTAL: /14

Comprehension Quiz

Choose the word or phrase that correctly completes each statement.

13. _____ refers to the entire message that the writer is trying to send through his story through the use of characterization, action, and images.

    a) Setting   **b) Theme**   **c) Resolution**

14. _____ _____ are communication devices.

    a) Graphic organizers   **b) Telephone calls**   **c) Post offices**

15. The _____ of a story is the way a story gets told and who tells it.

    a) setting   **b) point of view**   **c) plot**

16. In the _____ person point of view, a character in the story is the narrator. This character is telling the story. The narrator uses the pronouns I, me, and we.

    a) first   **b) second**   **c) third**

17. In the _____ person point of view, the story is being told by an outside observer (someone who is not in the story). The author uses the pronouns he, she, and they.

    a) first   **b) second**   **c) third**

18. _____ happens when an author mentions or hints at something that will happen later in the story.

    a) Flashback   **b) Foreshadowing**   **c) Irony**

19. _____ is an expression in which the intended meaning of the words is the direct opposite of their usual sense.

    a) Flashback   **b) Foreshadowing**   **c) Irony**

20. _____ happens when an object in a story, play, or movie stands for a feeling, idea, or concept.

    a) Symbolism   **b) Foreshadowing**   **c) Irony**

SUBTOTAL: **/8**

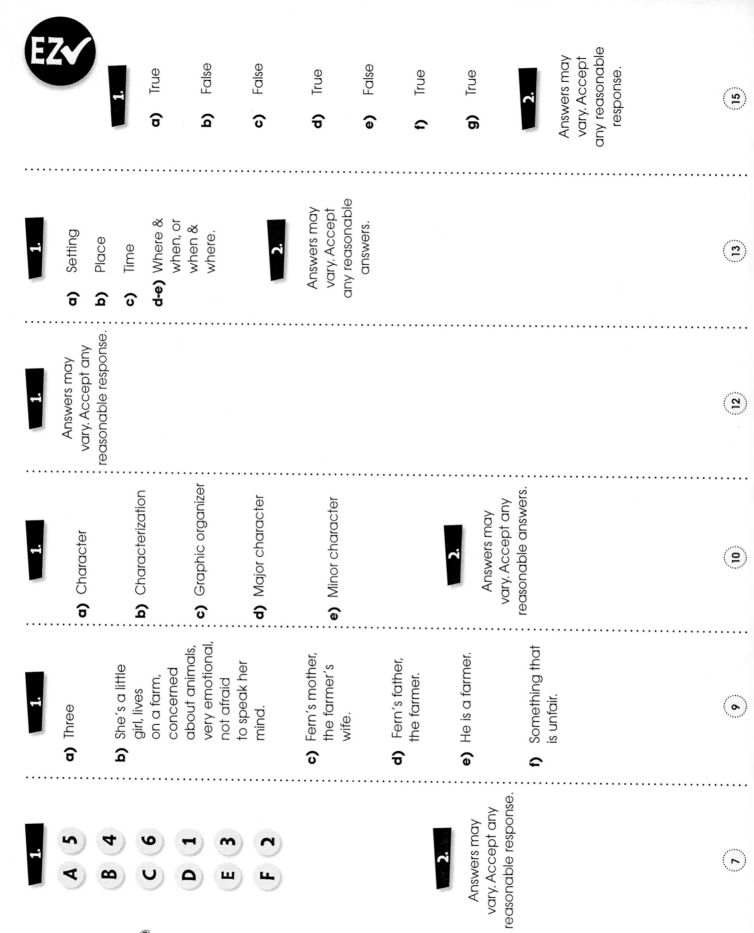

EZ✓

1.
a) True
b) False
c) False
d) True
e) False
f) True
g) True

2. Answers may vary. Accept any reasonable response.

15

1.
a) Setting
b) Place
c) Time
d-e) Where & when, or when & where.

2. Answers may vary. Accept any reasonable answers.

13

---

1. Answers may vary. Accept any reasonable response.

12

1.
a) Character
b) Characterization
c) Graphic organizer
d) Major character
e) Minor character

2. Answers may vary. Accept any reasonable answers.

10

1.
a) Three
b) She's a little girl, lives on a farm, concerned about animals, very emotional, not afraid to speak her mind.
c) Fern's mother, the farmer's wife.
d) Fern's father, the farmer.
e) He is a farmer.
f) Something that is unfair.

9

1.
A 5
B 4
C 6
D 1
E 3
F 2

2. Answers may vary. Accept any reasonable response.

7

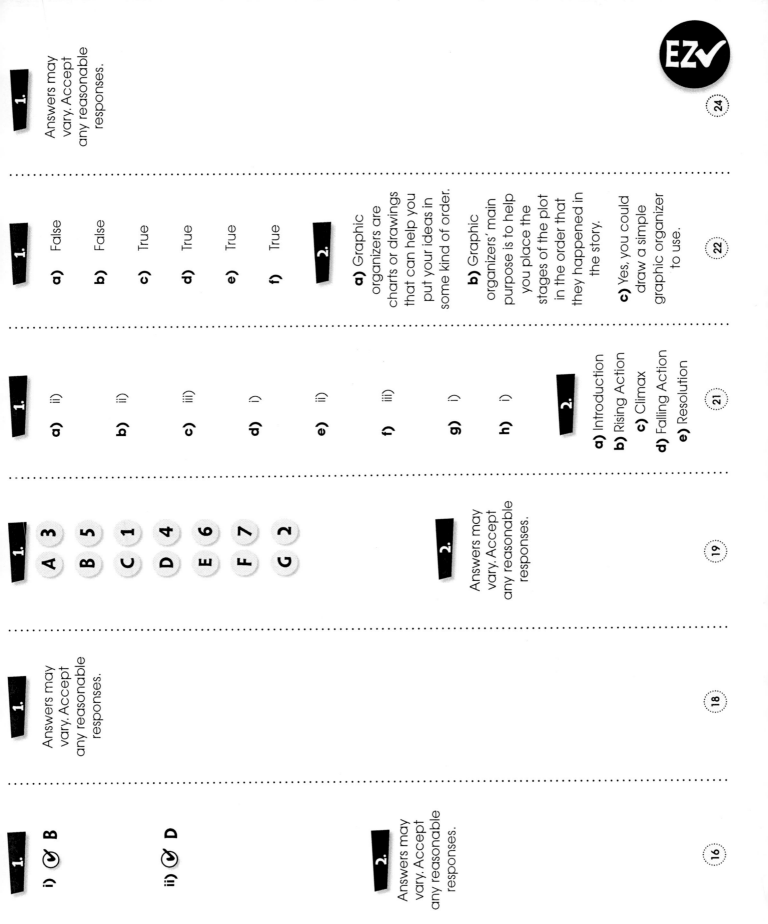

1.
Answers may vary. Accept any reasonable responses.

⟨24⟩

1.
a) False
b) False
c) True
d) True
e) True
f) True

2.
a) Graphic organizers are charts or drawings that can help you put your ideas in some kind of order.

b) Graphic organizers' main purpose is to help you place the stages of the plot in the order that they happened in the story.

c) Yes, you could draw a simple graphic organizer to use.

⟨22⟩

1.
a) ii)
b) ii)
c) iii)
d) i)
e) ii)
f) iii)
g) i)
h) i)

2.
a) Introduction
b) Rising Action
c) Climax
d) Falling Action
e) Resolution

⟨21⟩

1.
A 3
B 5
C 1
D 4
E 6
F 7
G 2

2.
Answers may vary. Accept any reasonable responses.

⟨19⟩

1.
Answers may vary. Accept any reasonable responses.

⟨18⟩

1.
i) ✓ B
ii) ✓ D

2.
Answers may vary. Accept any reasonable responses.

⟨16⟩

1.
a) ii)
b) iv)
c) i)
d) iii)

2. Answers may vary. Accept any reasonable responses.

(33)

1.
A 4
B 3
C 6
D 1
E 5
F 2

2.
a) Third person
b) First person
c) First person
d) Third person

(31)

---

1. Answers may vary. Accept any reasonable response.

(30)

1.
a) True
b) False
c) True
d) False

2. Answers may vary. Accept any reasonable response.

(28)

1.
a) The theme of any story is the main idea or point that the author is trying to tell the audience. The subject of a story is simply its main idea or the topic that the story is about.
b) An author can express the theme(s) of a story in four ways: (1) by the feelings of the main characters, (2) through the thoughts of the main characters, (3) through events of the story, and (4) through the actions of the characters.

2.
a) ii) "Saving today will help you tomorrow."
b) The Ant and the Grasshopper.

(27)

1.
a) Literary elements
b) Character
c) Setting
d) Aesop's Fables
e) Theme
f) Plot

2.
i) A, B
ii) B, C, D, F
iii) A, B, C, D, E, F
iv) A, B, E, F
v) A, B, E
vi) A, C, D

(25)

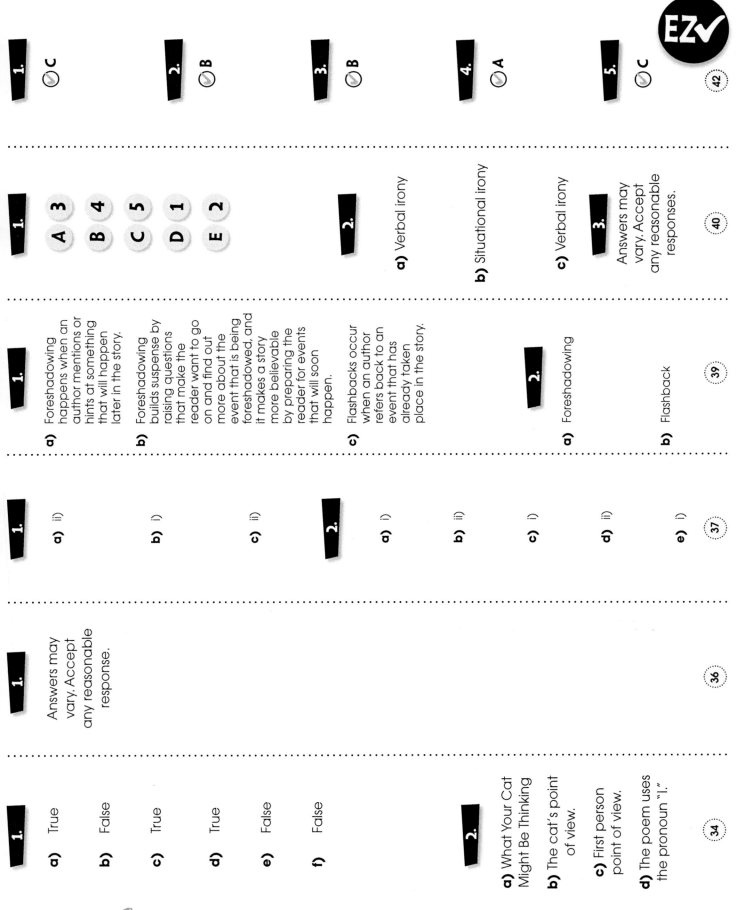

1.
- C

2.
- B

3.
- B

4.
- A

5.
- C

EZ✓

(42)

1.
- A 3
- B 4
- C 5
- D 1
- E 2

2.
a) Verbal irony
b) Situational irony
c) Verbal irony

3. Answers may vary. Accept any reasonable responses.

(40)

1.
a) Foreshadowing happens when an author mentions or hints at something that will happen later in the story.
b) Foreshadowing builds suspense by raising questions that make the reader want to go on and find out more about the event that is being foreshadowed, and it makes a story more believable by preparing the reader for events that will soon happen.
c) Flashbacks occur when an author refers back to an event that has already taken place in the story.

2.
a) Foreshadowing
b) Flashback

(39)

1.
a) ii)
b) i)
c) ii)

2.
a) i)
b) ii)
c) i)
d) ii)
e) i)

(37)

---

1. Answers may vary. Accept any reasonable response.

(36)

1.
a) True
b) False
c) True
d) True
e) False
f) False

2.
a) What Your Cat Might Be Thinking
b) The cat's point of view.
c) First person point of view.
d) The poem uses the pronoun "I."

(34)

13. b)
14. a)
15. b)
16. a)
17. c)
18. b)
19. c)
20. a)

49

1. T
2. F
3. T
4. F
5. T
6. T
7. F
8. T
9. F
10. T

11. Answers should include: introduction, rising action, climax, falling action, and resolution.

12. Climax is the "high point" of a story when the major conflicts end up in some kind of final showdown (a fight, an argument, physical action, or a very tense emotional moment). The climax is the point in the story where something CHANGES.

48

Word Search Answers

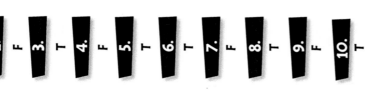

47

Across
1. Character
5. View
6. Setting
9. Plot
10. Falling
12. Introduction
13. Graphic
14. Aesops

Down
2. Action
3. Elements
4. Climax
7. Situation
8. Flashback
11. Irony

46

Character Analysis

• • • • • •   • • • • • •   • • • • •

Selection Title _____

Character:	Passages:
Words	
Actions	
Appearance	
Thoughts	
Effects on Other People	
Direct Characterization	
Analysis of Character	

Characterization

Dialogue
(What does the dialogue reveal about him or her?)

Physical Description
(What does he or she look like?)

Thoughts
(What is he or she thinking?)

Character Name:

Actions
(What do actions reveal about him or her? Include gestures, motions.)

Reactions of Others
(What do others think of him or her?)

Five Stages of Plot Development

1. _____

(Describes the characters and the setting of the story.)

5. _____

(A tying-up of all the loose ends left in the story.)

2. _____

(Conflicts are introduced, and readers find out more about the characters.)

4. _____

(Deals with the results of the climax.)

3. _____

(The "high point" of a story.)

Literary Devices CC1117

Theme Chart

Title	
Main Characters	
Main Conflict	
Main Theme	
Beginning of Theme	
Development of Theme	
Climax of Theme	
Resolution of Theme	